What Matters for Children and Families

what matters for children and families

ENGAGING SIX VITAL THEMES OF OUR FAITH

Frank Proctor, editor

UNITED CHURCH PRESS
CLEVELAND

United Church Press, 700 Prospect Avenue, Cleveland, Ohio 44115,
unitedchurchpress.com
© 2009 by United Church Press

This resource is a project developed under the leadership of Lutie O. Lee, Min-
ister for Children and Families in the Congregational Vitality and Discipleship
Ministry Team, Local Church Ministries. It has been produced in partnership
with The Pilgrim Press and Congregational Vitality and Discipleship Ministry
Team. Timothy Staveteig, publisher, The Pilgrim Press and UCC Resources,
Publications, Resources and Distribution, Local Church Ministries and David
Schoen, minister and team leader, Congregational Vitality and Discipleship
Ministry Team, Local Church Ministries.

Printed in the United States of America on acid-free paper

14 13 12 11 10 09   5 4 3 2 1

Library of Congress Cataloging-in-Publication Data

What matters for children and families : engaging six vital themes of our faith /
Frank Proctor, editor.
     p. cm.
   Includes bibliographical references.
   ISBN 978-0-8298-1864-2 (alk. paper)
   1. United Church of Christ—Doctrines. 2. Christian education--Home train-
ing. 3. Christian education of children. I. Proctor, Frank.
   BX9886.W43 2009   268'.85834—dc22
                                                        2009019673

contents

preface

Families, and the children that are part of them, matter to us in the United Church of Christ. This book is offered to families in the United Church of Christ as a spiritual gift to help us all share our love for this church with our children. It is a resource to help initiate conversations through which children will catch the vision and values of our denomination.

It is not a history book. It is not a list of the beliefs of one particular branch of the Christian family of churches. Instead, this book focuses on the core values held by people who find the life and traditions of the United Church of Christ to be a great blessing to their lives. It is about *What Matters* to us.

Eight writers, who represented several different family heritage groups, have collaborated to provide this resource for leaders of our congregations as well as for parents and caregivers. It is a vehicle or some suggestions about ways to trigger discussions about *What Matters* to those of us who call the United Church of Christ our spiritual home. There are Bible stories; questions for reflections, suggestions for reading children's literature that illustrate our core values, ideas for activities to do as a family and prayers written by our diverse writers.

In the United Church of Christ, children matter a great deal. We cherish their presence in worship. We involve them in the programs and projects of the whole church. We stand up for their education, health and welfare in our society. And we work at helping them adopt for themselves those religious traditions, concepts and attitudes that are important to us in the United Church of Christ.

We hope this work will find its way into the practice and habits of the Christian family—whether that might be within groups in congregations or in the personal surroundings of the home. We hope it will help our children begin to learn *What Matters*.

Acknowledgments

Grateful acknowledgments for coming together to write this *What Matters for Children and Families* resource go to: Ms. Lutie O. Lee, Minister for Children and Families, Congregational Vitality and Discipleship Team, Local Church Ministries, Rev. Joanne Bogart of Denver, Colorado, Mrs. Sol Cotto of Philadelphia, Pennsylvania, Mrs. Ruth Hainsworth of Riverside, Rhode Island, Rev. Dr. Divina Himaya of Claremont, California, Dr. Alison G. Johnson of Chicago, Illinois, Rev. Bennie Liggins of Montgomery, Alabama, Rev. Esther Rendon Thompson of Womelsdorf, Pennsylvania. Great appreciation goes to Gloria Otis for her work on this resource.

Rev. Frank Proctor, editor

Introduction

"Let us bake cookies and feed the protesters!" suggested the Church School teacher to the children at Simi Valley United Church of Christ (UCC) in Simi Valley, California. "Let us talk to the protesters and find out why they are upset that we are supporting Liliana?" declared the youth leader to the youth.

Exposing our children and youth to life's engagement in the real world begins the process of faith formation in their hearts and minds. In 2007, the above scenario described one of the scenes Liliana and her family experienced while worshiping on their first Sunday at Simi Valley UCC. For years to come, the children and youth of Simi Valley UCC will look back on the drama that unfolded before their very eyes! To some of them, it might have been the experience of faith being caught than taught! The Church School teacher and youth leader modeled what Micah 6:8 says, ". . . What does the Lord require of you, but to do justice, and to love kindness, and to walk humbly with your God?"

When Immigration and Customs Enforcement (ICE) officials entered Liliana's home in Oxnard, CA with deportation order for her, she sought help from The Sanctuary Movement. Currently, she lives with her baby, Pablito, at the Simi Valley UCC parsonage while attorneys with the Center for Human Rights and Constitutional Law and a local attorney seek legal options for her to remain with her family. On their first Sunday worship with her husband and two other children, there were demonstrators representing pro and anti-immigrant groups. Outside the church, people yelled on bullhorns. Initially, an anti-immigrant group held weekly protests; now it is monthly. Since the time Simi Valley UCC voted to become a sanctuary for imperiled immigrants, the church family has become the faith community for Liliana and her family. For over a year, members have religiously taken turns, around the clock, to accompany her at night in the parsonage. The able leadership of the pastor, Rev. Dr. June Goudey provided a peaceful, prophetic witness to the community. This is an expression of what intergenerational faith entails; sowing the seeds for faith formation. Young and old, men and women, children and youth, everyone participates in perfect harmony upholding the still-speaking God to the Simi Valley community.

The ever formation of faith in our lives keeps going just like the flow of Niagara Falls. Some will have a well-grounded foundation; others will have a bumpy formation; and still others will have a vague notion of faith. A hospice chaplain summed it succinctly when she described that in her experience, dying patients who had a deep foundation of their faith, Christian or not, die well and with grace. They seem to have a peaceful countenance as they approach the final chapter of their lives. Turning her description into a positive notion of faith, this line came to being: *"Faith supports every breath of life."*

To Whom and How Will this Resource be Used?

This is a resource for parents and Christian educators. Although we realize that some communities of faith might not have Christian educators on staff, it would be preferred if a Christian educator could teach parents and caregivers how to share and nurture children's faith formation. Once parents have gained comfortable engagement with this resource, only then are they going to use them with their children.

In a book by Marjorie Thompson, *Family the Forming Center*, she outlines six foundational practices that shape the sacred shelter of families: presence, acceptance, accountability, hospitality, affirmation and forgiveness. These concepts are imbedded all over the pages, from the introduction, biblical passages, questions for reflection, suggested family activities, the prayers, United Church of Christ identity pieces as it relates to children, and to the children's literature. If this resource were seriously utilized, Thompson's foundational practices for faith formation would be taking roots in the lives of children and families.

The themes are patterned after the *What Matters* literature produced by Congregational Vitality Initiative, namely:

- We are people of God's extravagant welcome.
- We belong to Christ.
- We are one at the baptism and the table.
- We are people of covenant.
- We thank God by working for a just and loving world.
- We listen for a still-speaking God.

Before each theme is introduced, a United Church of Christ identity piece is provided and at the end of each chapter information on, "Children Matters in the UCC" is shared. A Bible passage is chosen that resonates with the theme and questions for reflection are included. Suggested family activities follow and the family time ends with a prayer. In another setting, a children's book that highlights or relates to the message of the "What Matters" theme can be read to the children. This can be done as a bedtime story or during quiet time. The resource material is written for younger and older children up to 12 years of age. Parents might organize family activities differently after they have become comfortable on how to use the resource with their children. What's most important is that parents are given the tools to engage faith formation with their children.

Reading the Scriptures

The United Church of Christ tradition of engaging children with Bible stories encourages openness of mystery and wonder. This approach will draw them "to discover what they can from God's stories now, knowing intuitively that there is always more to be discovered later."[1] The completion of the Bible did not end God's revelation. More is yet to come! "This attitude sets the stage for a lifelong exploration of Scripture rather than the collection of right facts and answers"[2] from the Bible. Consequently, this approach, doesn't "drill" our children on memorizing Bible verses. The approach, however, nurtures them to a faith that is open to God's unsuspecting surprises. Let children have the joy of discovery by being invited to enter into the stories. Then give them the time to make their own discoveries. "Never place a period, where God has placed a comma," has become the slogan of the United Church of Christ in recent years. (This is a direct quote from the comedienne Gracie Allen to her husband, comedienne George Burns.)

Setting the stage of mystery and wonder in discovering God's truths invites children to engage in "wonder questions." Wondering magnetizes our children to be drawn to Scriptures. Encouraging them to wonder gives the notion that adults are child-friendly. They will feel confident to enter God's stories to find meaning and direction in their young lives. Because of the UCC tradition of openness in engaging children with "God-talk," parents should consider selected contemporary children's literature to provide another venue to discover precious realities suited for their children. Through these stories "children seem able to process deep realities at an affective level before they can conceptualize the truths. To give the great realities of the faith to children, those realities must be in story form,"[3] whether coming from Bible stories or children's literature. Children need time to wonder about the mystery of their young Christian faith.

Children's Literature

Engaging children with biblical narratives and linking the theme with children's literature will inspire and stimulate their appreciation for stories written for their age level. This resource not only anchors faith formation through the Scriptures, but also through contemporary children's literature. The children's literature can be found in libraries or bookstores.

God speaks in mysterious ways. There is no fixed formula how God speaks to us. Sometimes, readers encounter a higher presence through engagement with a contemporary story written for children or adults. A United Church of Christ Southern California clergy once said her defining moment of becoming a Christian happened while reading Tolstoy's *War and Peace*. She encountered Jesus! May the interactive time you will spend with your children through reading Scriptures and children's literature, deepen your faith and that of your children with a living God.

Honoring diversity

Time evolves. We have come a long way. The United Church of Christ is intentional in honoring diverse voices, where in the past, "there was no room in the inn." A group of diverse writers convened together for a week in February 2008 to write Faith Formation resource materials. The group was so diverse that during the first day of the writers' workshop, differences of perspective were quite obvious. But no one judged one another as being "wrong" in explaining or expressing their "out of the box" perspective, apart from the dominant culture's worldviews. Everyone accepted each other. As days went by, each person was changed. Learning about others' lived realities; others' moans and groans became our own. God was still speaking in our midst! As one writer wrote in the Association of United Church Educators' (AUCE) newsletter, "As our time together came to a close, we talked about what made this experience so sacred for each of us. We were able to identify that, for the first time, none of us felt as though he or she was serving as a token representative of a particular group. All of us had found the freedom to be fully and authentically ourselves together. We also experienced the immeasurable gift of seeing ourselves through the other eyes. For me, this was the first time in my life that I had to live and work with the label 'Euro,' assigned to me by others without my input or permission. This label has become a lasting gift and continues to reveal in excruciating clarity the labels I so casually assign to others." Even after the workshop concluded, the group continued to gather together in Church House, the national offices of the United Church of Christ, or in the lobby of the Radisson Hotel.

1 we are people of God's extravagant welcome

Introduction

The United Church of Christ has engaged in a campaign to let the broader society become better aware of the values and attractions of our churches. In a specific campaign of television advertising known as the "God is Still Speaking" campaign, the UCC has sought to let others know that we are a people of extravagant welcome. The most recent ads suggest, with the old children's song, you can open the door and see ALL the people.

The United Church of Christ is the first Protestant denomination in the USA to ordain an African-American, a woman as well as the first to ordain gays and lesbians.

In the United Church of Christ (UCC), we have the strong conviction that it is God's role to judge the quality of one's faith. We believe that it is inappropriate for the church or any individual to assume the role as judge. In our society, we often assume people have certain convictions of faith that are different from ours because of one's race, gender, cultural heritage, language or accent, and family configuration. In the UCC, we are called to rise above pre-judging people and to practice behaviors so others who are different from us feel welcomed and cherished.

Similarly, we believe that the Holy Scriptures clearly teach that "God loves the (whole) world which includes all human beings who are the creation of a loving God. Throughout the life and ministry of Jesus Christ, all people have been accepted regardless of age, tongue, or race. This principle of acceptance and welcome applies regardless of religious experience, life challenges or personal convictions. Our God is a welcoming, inclusive God. Therefore, the work of the church is to be welcoming and open to all people.

This principle of extravagant welcome applies to a variety of family configurations. In today's American society, there is no "typical" family structure that is seen as the norm or the model for families. Families may be blended. Families may include more than two adults. Some have extended families all in one abode. Some families involve parents of the same sex; grandparents head other families. The expectation of what constitutes a whole and wholesome family has variations between folks of differing cultural heritages. The UCC tries to welcome groups of folks who define themselves as a family regardless of structure.

Similarly, all children are cherished and welcomed in the UCC. This includes children living in broken families and with medical, mental or physical differences. Baptized children are welcomed to take communion in most UCC congregations. Children are protected from risky and dangerous situations by policies that guarantee their safety in church. Some churches have been practicing intergenerational worship. Children are given parts in a regular Sunday worship not because it is Christmas or Easter. The style of how children are included, however, has some variation in different portions of the country. Likewise, there may be a variety of ways children are taught about faith or included in whole church community events because of one's cultural heritage or traditions. In the overall picture, the UCC strives to practice extravagant welcome to all, no matter where they are in life's journey.

Whatever the family configuration, churches seek to provide programs for children of all ages and to support parents in their responsibilities as teachers of faith. There are organized religious educational programs for children, youth and adults in most churches especially in medium sized and large congregations. The nature of UCC churches, that of being autonomous, allows churches to be free to choose programs for children and families that best fits their theological views. Thus, the UCC gives local churches the freedom to be able to welcome children and families that choose them.

Honoring an Extravagant Welcome to Native Americans

The special honorees in this resource are the Native Americans. They were the natives who already inhabited this vast land prior to the coming of the Puritans and Colonists. In the past, the traditions and practices they observed were labeled as evil and demonic. Toni Buffalo, a Lakota Indian will share one tradition that, in the past, had been given the label, "sweat lodge experience." This is a term that is offensive to Native Americans. They call it *inipi* (purification) tradition; a sacred ceremony. When Toni was asked if she could share a very meaningful traditional Native American practice that could be a resource on faith formation, she could not contain her joy for being asked to share their sacred tradition.

Inipi (Purification) Tradition

"Hello, my name is Toni Buffalo and I am a Lakota woman from South Dakota. Our family is a blended family—his, hers, and ours. I am the youngest of 13 children, although I was raised with only ten of my siblings.

Both of my parents were recovering alcoholics and were very involved with Alcoholics Anonymous. I think I knew the 12 steps before I ever learned the Ten Commandments. I grew up thinking that God's real name was "The Higher Power." I was not baptized, as my parents couldn't agree at which church I should join, so they decided to let me make the choice when I was older.

Regretfully, since alcoholism can be hereditary, I also became involved with alcohol and drugs. Even during those days, I did not realize that my faith was forming through this "Higher Power" that my parents always talked about. I entered into treatment when I was 18 years old and then found out for myself how very important a "Higher Power" is in one's life, especially one struggling to find herself. After about six months of sobriety, I was told to give a name to my "Higher Power." I had a non-native friend who was a "born again" Christian. This friend told me that if I wanted sobriety I needed to accept Jesus and say the sinner's prayer; then everything would change. I did so and waited for a jolt of something to change me; to let me know I, too was reborn. It didn't feel right. I was also told that I no longer needed my Lakota culture or spirituality because it was pagan and if I really believed in Jesus, I would readily walk away from this.

One evening I got on my knees and prayed. I prayed, "God, Tunkasila, Jesus, or whoever you are, please help me know how to pray to you, show me your way." Not long after that prayer I met one of our elders who instructed me in our old way of prayer called purification (*inipi*); Sundance ceremony; or vision quest.

When I first went into our *inipi*, it was explained to me that coming into the lodge was like being in our mother's womb and when we leave, we are born again, all new and purified. (Hmmm, born again/reborn—heard that somewhere before!) All our worries, concerns, negative thoughts and feelings were to be left there and we would leave that sacred place with a purified mind, body, and spirit.

Inside the round lodge I felt safe, secure, and a warmth that one would feel in the loving arms of their mother. As heated red rocks were brought in and placed into the pit in the center of the lodge—you are the old ones, the *inyans* (rocks) and how they gave of themselves to be heated so we could purify ourselves. The cedar that is placed on each rock sets the mind frame to not only breathe in the healing smell from this tree, but to begin the cleansing. Then the water is brought in and the first few dippers are poured as thanks is given for the *Mne Wakan* (sacred water). Mne Wakan gives life to all living things and refreshes, renews, and restores one's mind, body, and spirit.

The door is closed and darkness envelops you and though you are next to someone, it is still just you and the Creator of the universe. You are free to pour out anything and everything you feel you need to share with our Creator. God is here! You learn how humbling it is to be a mere human, not being able to give anything back to the natural elements you are using: the wood, rocks, fire, and water. It reconnects your whole being with this beautiful creation that God has made and has given to us to care for. You leave this sacred ceremony, truly renewed, refreshed, and reborn. This is how I learned about spirituality and how my faith was formed.

I had not come to know Jesus Christ until I met my husband, Byron Buffalo. My previous experiences with Christianity had not been very positive. I was continually told that to be more Christ-like, I had to give up who God made me to be. I experienced physical abuse from those who were to be examples of Christ. I wanted nothing to do with that type of Christianity.

My husband introduced me to a man named Jesus and he showed me what Jesus had done in his life. By example, he showed me the love of Christ, of his unbelievable mercy and how that included me as I am. I came to know and to love Christ and have experienced his renewal; his refreshment. He truly is the living water. Today I continue to be who I am: God blessed me to be a Lakota woman. He introduced his son, and Jesus and I need not give up one to be the other. I am a child of the Almighty God, the Creator of all.

Native Americans approach the world wholistically. Toni's original invitation was to describe their *inipi* tradition. She, however, declined to describe the *inipi* without sharing her faith journey. Without giving context, it would have stripped her tradition of its meaning and sacredness. It would have no music to their ears.

Biblical Foundation

A. For Younger Children: Read Luke 19:1–10
"Jesus Welcomes Zacchaeus"

This is one of the endearing stories about Jesus' compassion for the least appreciated folks. Zacchaeus was one of them. Instead of joining the crowd who loathed Zacchaeus, Jesus invited himself to Zacchaeus' house. In spite of your reputation, wouldn't you be shocked if Jesus had singled you out in the crowd? During Jesus' time, a person with Zacchaeus' profession was considered a sinner because he collected taxes for Rome. Jesus must have a compelling personality because at the end of his visit, Zacchaeus was a changed man. He told Jesus, "Look Lord! Here and now I give half of my possessions to the poor, and if I have cheated anybody out of anything, I will pay back four times the amount." Jesus welcomes even a man like Zacchaeus.

Suggestions for Wondering about this Story with Young Children:

- I wonder if there are people that our family thinks are bad; just as people thought of Zacchaeus.

- Have my children witness me behaving poorly by not welcoming a person who had done similar things like Jesus?

- Have I been a good example to my children? If I have had some moments of weakness in my behavior, now is the time to say, "I'm sorry" to them. It is not easy to walk our talk. If Jesus came to visit, what would I do with my children? Was there ever a time when the church treated us like Zacchaeus and elbowed us to the back of the crowd or group?

- Are we concerned that our children are not welcoming of others who are different from them?

- Have you ever felt you were too short, too young, too loud, or too silly to be in church? Or some other place where adults were in charge?

- Did anyone ever treat you as if you were not wanted?

- Can you think of a time when you were too shy to speak to a guest or visitor in church?

- Can you imagine what Jesus would say to your family if he came to dinner? Would he like your family? Would he like everyone in the family?

- Would Jesus only talk with the adults in your family? Or, would he talk with everyone?

- Is there a game you play at school that is specifically designed to push people out of the group (like musical chairs, a spelling bee, etc.)? How did you feel when you played that game?

B. For Older Children: Read Luke 15:11–32 "The Parable of the Lost Son"

After the younger son squandered his inheritance and asked to be taken back by his father, without hesitation the father extended his extravagant welcome to his lost son. The son's homecoming was treated like a hero's welcome! The father said, "Quick! Bring the best robe and put it on him. Put a ring on his finger and sandals on his feet. Bring the fattened calf and kill it. Let's have a feast and celebration. For this son of mine was dead and is alive again, he was lost and is found."

The older son heard the excitement and upon inquiring learned the party was in honor of his brother's return, he was not a happy camper. He got angry and refused to join in the celebration. He felt it was not fair for his father to give his brother a party after he had wasted his inheritance. Afterall, he had been the faithful son helping his father at home. Yet, his father had never given him a party, not even killing a small goat for him. His father reasoned this brother of his has returned from the dead. He has been lost, but now is found.

For Parents—Suggestions for Wondering about this Story with Older Children:

To some children, this passage might cause them to have mixed feelings. Perhaps, it would remind them of your actions.

- Did you respond with extravagant welcome; showing unconditional love to your rebellious son or daughter?

- If you were indeed overjoyed and threw a party, did you wonder if other children felt jealous? What did you do?

- Do you advocate extravagant welcome to the marginalized and disadvantaged people in your community?

- Do you wonder if you have demonstrated this stand to your children?

- What is your view of illegal immigrants; do you welcome them in our country? Or, do you fight for them, providing them a sanctuary?

- In troubled times with your pre-teen/s, do you feel close to God in prayer or alienated from God? Why?

For older children:

- Have you ever felt that your parents do not understand what you are saying to them or want from them?

- Has there ever been a time when you felt excluded in your family? Have you felt alone or unwelcome even in your own home?

- Have you tried praying to God for guidance and support during such times?

- Do you know of other people, like the pastor of your church or a schoolteacher to whom you could share your concerns?

- Have you welcomed someone in your home or your neighborhood? What did you say? What did you do together?

- Was that a meaningful experience for you? Why? Or why not?

- What does your family do with other families?

- What do you do with other young people your age that makes you feel you are all children of God?

Suggested activities for families with children:

1. Think of a way your family can show extravagant welcome — be a greeter at your church or when someone new visits your church, invite him or her to dinner.

2. Organize a cultural heritage celebration in your children's school.

3. Speak to your City Council about ways to welcome new immigrants in your community.

4. Adopt a tradition in your family that comes from a cultural heritage that is different from your own:

   —use the piñata

   —learn to cook Asian food or African American soul food

   —celebrate three Kings or Las Posadas

Family Prayer

> *Dear God,*
> *May we always be faithful to shower extravagant welcome to all children now only in our own nation but also around the world. In Jesus name, Amen.*

Suggested children's literature to link the theme: "We are people of God's extravagant welcome"

For young children:

Ambrosia by Dan Manalang, Illustrations by Nichole Wong, Hawthorne: Flip Publishing, 2005, ISBN: 0-9769342-0-5. To order visit: *www.Amazon.com.*

Summary

This is a story that would address welcoming diversity. A story of fruits has come to life about a grumpy grape, a fresh peach, a pompous pineapple, and a humble coconut. At first the fruits despised the hairy coconut only to find out how delicious is the taste of the coconut! This charming rhyme addresses the sensitive subject of prejudice. It is a poetic story that teaches children to see the beauty in diversity.

Questions to engage young children about the story:

1. I wonder how the coconut felt when someone said, "It's certainly not one of us?"

2. Have you ever seen another child treated like the "coconut" in your school or group? How did that feel?

3. How do you think Jesus would feel about the way the other fruits treated the coconut? What would he teach us today?

4. What would you say to the coconut to help him feel better?

5. Have you ever been told by your parents to be afraid of someone you met who you did not know? Do you think that was right or wrong? Why?

Don't Call Me Special by Pat Thomas, Illustrations by Lesley Harker, Hauppauge: Barron's Educational Series, Inc. 2000, ISBN -10: 0-7641-2118-9, ISBN-13: 978-0-7641-2118-0. To order visit: *www.barronseduc.com*

Summary

This is a story that would address welcoming differently abled people. This delightful picture book explores questions and concerns about being differently abled in a simple and reassuring way. Younger children can find out what being differently abled is, and learn how people cope with their abilities to live happy and full lives.

Questions to engage young children about the story

1. Have you wondered how differently abled children come to be? What happened?

2. Have you wondered what it would be like to have a conversation with a differently abled child? Will there be a difference?

3. What would be your extravagant welcome to differently abled children?

4. If you are a differently abled child, what do you want to say to other children?

King & King by Linda de Haan & Stern Nijland, Berkeley/Toronto: Tricycle Press, 2000, ISBN: 1-58246-061-2. To order visit: *www.tenspeed.com*.

Summary

This is a story that would address welcoming gays, lesbians, bisexuals, and transgendered people. The queen decrees that it's time for the prince to marry and the search is on! Princesses come from far and wide hoping to catch his eye. Will the prince be charmed by a magic act? Tantalized by arias? Mesmerized by the Miss from Mumbai? Do you want to know who caught the apple of his eye? Read the book to find out!

Questions to engage children about the story:

1. Sometimes it is confusing when you are told that you are to only fall in love with a boy if you are a girl and with a girl if you are a boy. But in this story another prince caught the eye of the prince! Do you wonder about that?

2. What would Jesus say to this? Would he show an extravagant welcome to the new couple?

Sachiko Means Happiness by Kimiko Sakai, Illustrated by Tomie Arai, San Francisco: Children's Book Press, 1990, ISBN: 10:-0-89239-122-7. To order visit: *www.childrensbookpress.org* or call: 1-800-788-3123.

Summary

This is a story that would address welcoming senior citizens with Alzheimer's disease. A simply told story of young Sachiko's acceptance of her grandmother's Alzheimer's disease. It is illustrated in warm, sunset tones, with insets featuring traditional Japanese motifs. Over the years, Grandmother has changed, and now, childlike herself, she hardly recognizes her granddaughter Sachiko.

Questions to engage children about the story:

1. First of all, we must know what Alzheimer's disease is, it means some older folks lose the ability to remember or have difficulty in remembering. How did Sachiko shows her continued acceptance of her Grandmother?

2. Have you ever wondered how you would feel if you had difficulty remembering people's names or connecting the face with the name; things you did yesterday or a few seconds ago are already forgotten?

3. What extravagant welcome can we do for those with Alzheimer's Disease?

Cooper's Lesson by Sun Yung Shin, Illustrations by Kim Cogan, San Francisco: Children's Book Press, 2004, ISBN: 0-89239-193-6. To order visit: *www.childrensbookpress.org* or call: 1-800-788-3123.

Summary

This is a story that would address welcoming bicultural and bilingual children. Cooper has had about enough of being half and half. And he's certainly had enough of Mr. Lee, the owner of his neighborhood grocery store, speaking to him in Korean even though Cooper can't keep up. Why can't things be simple? Why can't he just be one thing or the other. Before long he realizes that the question of who we are is never simple—whether you talk about it in English or in Korean. Kim Cogan's richly hued oil paintings perfectly complement this story of identity and intergenerational friendship.

Questions to engage children about the story

1. Cooper had trouble having to be both at the same time, speaking English and Korean. Why can't he just be one or the other? Is it possible to just forget the other half of your identity? Or is it possible to keep both at the same time? What might be the benefits to be both?

2. Can you imagine what children and youth, in this situation, must deal with everyday?

3. Can you imagine what might be the pluses and minuses of being a bicultural and bilingual child?

I Don't Have Your Eyes by Carrie A. Kitze, Illustrations by Rob Williams, Warren: EMK Press, 2003, ISBN: 10: 0-9726244-2-2, ISBN: 13: 978-0-97262-442-8. To order visit: *www.borders.com* or *www.barnesandnoble.com.*

Summary

This is a story that would welcome adopted children and adoptive parents. This beautifully illustrated and uplifting book helps to create the intimate bond that is so important as a child discovers what family really is. While others may notice the physical differences, there are so many ways we can celebrate the commonality that makes us belong. This is a simple exploration of outside difference, inside sameness for young children in preschool or early elementary. We don't look the same on the outside, but in our hearts, we are the same.

Questions to engage children about the story

1. How did the writer make the readers—adopted or not—appreciate their moms and dads?

2. Can you imagine how it might feel to learn that you are adopted?

3. While biological parents may have reasons why they chose not to raise their children, it must be a rewarding thought for adopted children to know that they have been chosen by others to be loved. What do you think about that?

An Angel Just Like Me by Mary Hoffman, Illustrations by Cornelius Van Wright & Ying-Hwa Hu, London: Frances Lincoln Children's Books, 2007, ISBN: 978-1-84507-733-4. To order visit: www.*franceslincoln.com.*

Summary

This is a story that would address welcoming diversity. It is nearly Christmas, and Tyler's family is putting up the decorations. But when Tyler picks up the broken Christmas-tree angel, he can't help to ask, "Why are they always pink? Aren't there any black angels?" It's a question no one can answer. And when Tyler goes shopping for a black angel, he can't find a single one—until he tells his friend Carl, the problem . . . .

Questions to engage children about the story:

1. Have you ever wondered if God made angels in all races and ethnicities?

2. If people are made in God's image, and you now know that angels had been historically made to symbolize one race, what

are your thoughts about this?

3. Wouldn't you have searched for an angel that looked like you too?

4. How would we welcome diversity in the churches and schools?

Grandma and Me at the Flea by Juan Felipe Herrera, Illustrations by Anita De Lucio-Brock, San Francisco: Children's Book Press, 2002, ISBN -10: 0-89239-171-5. To order visit: *www.childrensbookpress.org* or call: 1-800-788-3123.

Summary

This is a story that would address welcoming our extended families. Every Sunday Juanito helps his grandma sell old clothes at the *remate*, the flea market. Juanito and his friends take part in Grandma's vision of the flea market as a place for helping and sharing as they romp from booth to sunny booth.

Questions to engage children about the story:

1. Juanito is close to his grandma. Do you have a favorite grandma like Juanito?

2. Juanito has so much fun going out with grandma. Are grandmas and grandpas fun?

Two Mrs. Gibsons by Toyomi Igus, Illustrations by Daryl Wells, San Francisco: Children's Book Press, ISBN: 0-89239-170-7. To order visit: *www.childrensbookpress.com* or call: 1-800-788-3123.

Summary

This is a story that would address welcoming mixed-race families. In this tender celebration of family and heritage, the author pays special tribute to her Japanese mother and African American grandmother. Daryl Wells' art lovingly highlights the differences between the two Mrs. Gibsons and the joys of growing up in a mixed-race family.

Questions to engage children about the story

1. Have you ever wondered how it might feel to be born into a family that represented different races and ethnicities—all with different skin colors—brown and yellow, black and white living under one roof?

2. Do you go to a school where mixed race children or children from the global community attend?

3. How about your church? Do you go to a multiracial and multicultural church? Have you ever wondered about this?

CHILDREN MATTER in the UCC . . . children of all abilities, with different learning styles, diverse cultural heritages or experiences, or varieties of family configurations are welcomed and addressed in materials published by the UCC. Our faith formation or Christian Education programs and resources seek to teach our children how to become more comfortable and welcoming with people who are different from one's self.

"Faith supports every breath of life."

2 we belong to Christ

Introduction

"Here is the church, here is the steeple, open the door and see all the people."
"All the people are welcome into the United Church of Christ."

(A children's song)

To say "We belong to Christ" is an amazing and powerful statement. It sounds like saying, "We belong to the Y" or "We belong to the Boys and Girls Club," but it's not the same at all. Belonging to any club or organization involves only a part of our lives; a part of who we are. We choose to join because we think we'll enjoy the activities and benefits of membership the organization offers, like swimming at the Y or after school programs at the Boys and Girls Club.

Belonging to Christ is not like belonging to a club. It involves all of who we are and it touches every part of our lives. Belonging to Christ is not a one time event, but instead is a process that unfolds over a lifetime. Belonging to Christ means living everyday in the way Jesus taught his disciples over 2000 years ago, that still speaks to us today. Belonging to Christ is belonging to God with all of who we are all the time, no matter what.

To say, "We belong to Christ" in the United Church of Christ is a very core statement of our identity, just like it would be in any Christian church. What is unique in the United Church of Christ is how we define "we." When we say "we," it truly means everyone and anyone. No one is excluded from the "we" because of the color of their skin or where they live or where they came from or what their health is or what they've done or not done, or who they choose to love. Everyone is the "we" in "We belong to Christ" in the United Church of Christ.

Children are open to exploring what it means to know that they belong to Christ. This exploration can happen at home in many ways as well as at church.

Biblical Foundation

A. *For younger children: Read John 10:11–16 "Jesus, the Good Shepherd"*

In this story Jesus is using the image of a shepherd and his sheep to illustrate his relationship with those who belong to him. Just like the sheep instinctively know the shepherd; those who belong to Christ know what it is to be loved unconditionally by God.

Suggestions for wondering about this story with young children:

Jesus beckons us to belong to him in a gentle and persuasive way.

- Where have you found yourself responding to Jesus' invitation?

- What would you say to Jesus?

- What would it be like to hear Jesus calling your name?

- What would his voice sound like?

- Would it be soft and gentle or strong and confident or something else altogether?

- What would you say to Jesus? Would you ask a question or just talk to him?

B. For older children: Read I Corinthians 12:12–21; 27 "Members of the Body of Christ"

For just as the body is one and have many members, and all the members of the body, though many are one body, so it is with Christ. For in the one Spirit we were baptized into one body—Jews or Greeks, slave or free—and we all made to drink of one Spirit.

Indeed, the body does not consist of one member, but of many. If the foot would say, "Because I am not a hand, I do not belong to the body," that would not make it any less a part of the body. And if the ear would say, "Because I am not an eye, I do not belong to the body," that would not make it any less a part of the body. If the whole body were an eye, where would the hearing be? If the body was all hearing, where would the sense of smell be? But, as it is, God arranged the members in the body, each of them, as God chose. If all were a single member, where would the body be? As it is, there are many members, yet one body. The eye cannot say to the hand, "I have no need of you," nor again the head to the feet,

"I have no need of you." Now you are the body of Christ and individual members of it.

Suggestions for wondering about this narrative with older children:

Apostle Paul is using the human body as a metaphor to explain how everyone is equally important as followers of Christ.

- Invite your child to draw one of Paul's illustrations of a person as a giant eyeball or ear or nose. This may provoke some giggles and that's okay.

- Ask your child to imagine what it would be like to try to live as a giant eyeball or ear or nose.

- What would it be like to see everything, but not be able to do anything else?

- After imagining together for a bit, explain to your child the truth of Paul's example that we do need all of the parts of the body working together.

- Encourage your child to think about what happens when a part of the body is hurt or injured.

- If necessary, point out that when one part of the body is not working due to illness or injury or some other reason, the body naturally compensates by using the remaining parts differently.

- Ask your child in what ways this is like the church.

Suggested activities for families with children:

1. Watch movies and together, think about:

   FINDING NEMO—This classic Disney movie explores the importance of belonging through the story of fishes. A father's amazing quest to find his lost son.

WHALE RIDER—This extraordinary film set in Papua, New Guinea tells the story of a young girl's desire to belong to her community in the way she feels she needs to be, the resistance she encounters, and ultimately overcomes in an amazing way.

2. Experience what it is to be part of the body of Christ by joining members of your church as a volunteer at a local food pantry or soup kitchen. These sites usually have tasks for every age, but it will be advisable to check in advance if you have children who are not yet of school age.

3. Arrange to visit an elderly neighbor or nursing home. This will remind them that they still belong to Christ. In advance of your trip, children can create "thinking of you" cards or drawings to leave as a reminder of their visit.

4. Explore belonging in a wider context by researching other churches in locations very different from your own through the ucc.org website. Contact the church for more information about the congregation and its community, including the possibility of having a "pen pal" from that congregation.

Family Prayer

Loving and embracing God,
Thank you for the gift of belonging to Christ. Help us to show our gratitude for this great gift as we live out our belonging each day in the ways you need us to. Thank you for loving us no matter what. Help us to live your love to others. In Jesus name, Amen.

Suggested children's literature to link the theme: "We belong to Christ"

For young children:

No David! by David Shannon, New York: The Blue Sky Press, 1998, ISBN 13: 978-0-590-93002-4. To order visit: *www.scholastic.com.*

Summary

This simply and beautifully illustrated book for young children shows in a powerful way, what it means to be loved no matter what.

Questions to engage young children about the story:

1. When have you felt like David; like you are always hearing "no"?

2. What things are you doing when you hear "no"?

3. How do you still know God loves you and your family?

Sneetches and Other Stories by Dr. Seuss, New York: Random House, 1961 ISBN: 0-394-80089-3. To order visit: *www.Amazon.com.*

Summary

"Sneetches" is one of several stories in this anthology of the Dr. Seuss stories.The Sneetches are identical to each other in every way except some have stars on their bellies and some do not. This difference, which starts to cause conflict, is turned upside down when an outsider visits and tries to help. His meddling ultimately shows that this one little difference doesn't really matter at all.

Questions to engage young children about the story:

1. When have you felt different from others or not part of a group? How did you handle it?

2. When have you made someone else feel left out? What could you have done differently?

3. What does Jesus say to people who feel left out?

If Jesus Came to Visit Me by Jill Roman Lord, Illustrations by Renee Graef, Nashville: CandyCanePress, 2004. ISBN: 0-8249-6568-X To order visit: *www.Amazom.com.*

Summary

This beautifully illustrated "board book" for young children contains a powerful message for all ages. Written in verse, the book is an account of what this child would do if Jesus came to visit her in her home. This touching account of how she would spend her day with Jesus is profound in its simplicity and a treasure for any family or church library.

Questions to engage young children about the story:

1. What snacks would you wish to offer Jesus?

2. What questions would you ask Jesus?

3. How do you think the little girl could show Jesus the gift of her heart?

4. Do you wonder about that?

For older children:

Barack Obama: Son of Promise, Child of Hope by Nikki Grimes, Illustrations by Bryan Collier, New York: Simon & Schuster Books for Young Readers, 2008, ISBN 13: 978-1-4169-7144-3. To order visit: *www.Amazon.com.*

Summary

Ever since Barack Obama was young, hope has lived inside of him. From the beaches of Hawaii to the streets of Chicago, from the jungles of Indonesia to the plains of Kenya, he has held on to hope. Even as a boy, Barack knew he wasn't quite like anybody else, but through his journeys he found the ability to listen to hope and become what he was meant to be: a bridge to bring people together. Barack Obama invites us to believe with him, to believe that every one of us has the power to change ourselves and change our world.

Questions to engage older children about the story:

1. Barack Obama struggled to belong constantly asking "Who am I?" He neither looks like his mother nor his father. Do you wonder what it is like to be a biracial child? Biracial means that your parents are of different nationalities. In the case of Barack Obama, his mother is European American while his father is African. Bi means two.

2. Do you wonder if Barack Obama's sense of belonging came from a church? Tears flowed down his cheeks. What sense of belonging do you think he felt?

CHILDREN MATTER in the UCC . . . we find many ways to help children learn to be responsible for others in our community and around the world; we collect money and design projects to support Heifer Project, One Great Hour of Sharing, local food pantries, and many other such work of mission and service.

"Faith supports every breath of life."

3 we are one at the baptism and the table

Introduction

"No matter who you are, or where you are on life's journey, you are welcome at the table of the Lord."

The United Church of Christ has, since its merger in 1957, invited all who worship to participate in the communion of bread and cup. There is no barrier for what you understand of the meaning of the Lord's Supper or your religious experience or faith heritage. You are welcome.

How would children and young families understand what the statement implies, "We are one at baptism and the table?" As members of the body of UCC affiliation, we are joined to Christ and to one another in the waters of baptism. Christ nurtures us in bread and wine. We hear and speak God's word together so that we may love God more deeply and serve neighbors more fully. Yes, we become one at baptism and the table!

We are joined to Christ and to one another in the waters of baptism. We baptize with water because John, the Baptist, baptized Jesus in water. It is a sign of God's love and a seal upon us that we are included in God's family of faith. Baptism is no ordinary experience. Rather, it is one of our deep acts of faith that we believe in the name of the Father, the Son, Jesus Christ, and the Holy Spirit. We die to sin and are raised to new life in Christ. It is a public confession with shared faith-community of believers that indeed we are one with them.

With infant and children baptism, their parents demonstrate that their children, from now on, will be nurtured in the same community of faith. Members of this community have a responsibility to mentor and nurture them along with their parents. Having been joined by Christ, there is no more east or west, south nor north but only one great fellowship of Christian love throughout the whole wide world. We forever proclaim entering into a covenant relationship with God.

Christ nurtures us in bread and wine. In taking the Lord's Supper, we give thanks for God's creating, redeeming power. We joyfully remember Christ's self-offering for us. We pray for the transforming power of the Holy Spirit. We are reconciled with Christ and one another experiencing a foretaste of Christ's heavenly realm even for brief moments during the partaking of the bread and wine. We celebrate the sacraments of the baptism and the table because they are signs and seals of new and abundant life in Christ.

The symbolic meaning, "There is no barrier for what you understand of the meaning of the Lord's Supper or what your religious experience or 'faith heritage' connects to the apostle's experience during Pentecost." The miracle of Pentecost is the unity of all nations. Divisions, whether among individuals, or among races, are the causes of the sin of the world: God created us that even in our differences we might enrich one another. Linguistic, racial and cultural differences are not meant to be a source of division, but elements of a universal harmony."[4] God with us, more revelation has yet to come for us to realize about who we really are in the beginning of time, that is, we're created to be one human race and in the image of God.[5]

What reinforced this belief of our oneness, but the life and teachings of Jesus, the Christ. We, in UCC hold his teaching that we are one at baptism and the table. "By freely eating with everyone, he breaks and challenges all the social taboos that keep people apart."[6] He advocated the "joy of common table fellowship with everyone."[7] That's why in the UCC, everyone is invited to partake of the bread and cup, young and old. The invitation is open to everyone; not only members. It's a great banquet! And, too, the individual act of baptizing children and adults mean we share our oneness to all Christians around the world. All Christians become connected to one another through the ritual of baptism. Whether baptism is through pouring, immersion, or sprinkling, there is meaning in the experience. "What matters is not our nationality, religion, or family name, but that we live God's will"[8] and thus, Jesus prayed, "that they may all be one." We are one at the baptism and the table.

Biblical Foundation

A. *For young children: Read Matthew 3:13–17 "Jesus Baptism"*

In this story of Jesus' baptism, John the Baptist wanted to be baptized by Jesus, but Jesus was determined John is the one appointed to baptize him. When Jesus was baptized, God's Spirit of love flew down to him. It looked like a dove. And a voice from heaven said, "This is my Son, whom I love; with him I am well pleased."

Suggestions for wondering about this story with young children:

- What do you wonder about this baptism of Jesus?

- In your own baptism, do you wonder if God would say a similar thing? Perhaps, God says, "I love you in Jesus. I'm pleased with you, too." Do you ever wonder if God is pleased with you?

- Do you remember the time when you were baptized and how did the water feel coming in contact with your skin? Can you remember to describe it?

Suggested family activities for younger children:

1. During your daily devotions at home or during another appropriate time, make a tradition to remember your child's baptism anniversary. Light a special candle to signify the baptism day.

2. Display pictures taken on the day of your child's baptism. Invite family and friends who were present at the baptism to celebrate a special dinner.

3. Have fun water-related activities to celebrate baptism: playing at a pool, enjoying cool drinks, splashing in a bath, watering plants, have children to pour water on each other's hands/feet while watering plants.

4. Visit your local library and borrow the movie, *The Lion King*. Follow the sequence of the "Circle of Life." The story of this movie suggests baptism. Have a family time to discuss the movie.

B. For older children: Read Mark 14:22–25 "The Lord's Supper"

The Lord's Supper commonly called, the Holy Communion or the communion of the bread and wine, is the most important ritual in the Christian tradition. This is the scene where Jesus started the tradition. He is saying that we eat the bread as remembrance of his body and drink the wine as remembrance of his blood. For UCC traditions, we celebrate the bread and cup as symbols not that we believe they really turned into real body and blood, but to thankfully remember Jesus' sacrifice and for our new and abundant life in Christ.

Suggestion for wondering about this narrative with children:

In the UCC, celebration of the bread and cup, the communion table, is open to everyone.

- Do you wonder about our openness? You need not be a bona fide member of the church to partake of the communion.

- Are all children really allowed to take communion? Every UCC church can decide that for itself.

  Jesus' inclusive attitude of inviting everyone to his banquet, rich and poor, friend and stranger, female and male, slave and free, and pure and impure, all sitting together at a table overturns the order of his society. We at the UCC also want to uphold this model by accepting everyone who wants to participate in taking Holy Communion.

- Do you wonder if churches really do this?

The more we experience the Lord's Supper, the more we are nurtured by the bread and wine. We experience the transforming power of the Holy Spirit as we witness how strangers are embraced in the table of our Jesus Christ.

Suggested family activities for older children:

1. If your church uses real bread for Communion, as a family, volunteer to bake the bread for Communion Sunday.

2. If your church tradition allows it, check to see if your family can prepare Communion by slicing the bread and pouring the juice or wine into the cups.

3. Visit your local library and borrow recommended DVDs about the life and teachings of Jesus Christ. The Mel Gibson movie, The Passion of the Christ, could be seen together as a family.

4. As a family start the tradition of going to church to observe Maundy Thursday, Good Friday, and Easter Sunday.

5. Try to wonder how Jesus would feel if we were rejected by others and not made to feel as if we belonged.

Family Prayer

Merciful and loving God,
Teach us to be appreciative of the gifts and talents that you have given to all
your children. Guide us through the power of your Holy Spirit to have peace
and understanding with all the different people that exist around the world
and in our own community. May we also walk the land like Jesus did—doing
deeds, healing the sick and oppressed, drinking and eating with them at the
table. In Jesus' name, we pray. Amen.

Suggested children's literature to link the theme: "We are one at the baptism and the table"

For younger children:

The Adventures of Connie and Diego Las Aventuras de Connie y Diego by Maria Garcia, Illustrations by Malaquias Montoya, San Francisco: Children's Book Press, ISBN: 0-89239-124-3. To order visit: *www.childrensbookpress.com* or call: 1-800-788-3123.

Summary

Rainbow-colored twins visit the homes of many different animals in their search for a place to belong.

Questions to engage young children about the story:

1. Let's wonder about the animal world. Like us, do you think the animals searched for a place to live where they could feel a sense of belonging? Did they find that community in the story? Describe it.

2. Are you a community where you live?

3. The community gathered in the ritual of baptism and embraces you as one of their own. As a family, discuss whether or not your church family acts as a "community"? Do you belong?

For older children:

Passage to Freedom: The Sugihara Story by Ken Mochizuki, Illustrations by Dom Lee, New York: Lee & Low Books Inc., 1997, ISBN:1-58430-157-0. To order visit: *www.leeandlow.com.*

Summary

This is an untold story about what one Japanese diplomat did at Kauna, Lithuania in 1940 just before the outbreak of World War II. It shares the story of what happened when Polish Jews, who were refugees, came to Sugihara's office to ask for visas to escape the Nazi soldiers. Kind-hearted Sugihara issued thousands of visas to give them passage to freedom. He did not sleep night and day. He issued visas even when his hands were sore from signing; time was of the essence. This is a story told through the eyes of Hiroki Sugihara, the son of Chiune Sugihara, the Japanese diplomat.

Suggestion to engage older children about the story:

1. Diplomat Sugihara welcomed the Polish Jews to his office. Do you think that they would be welcomed to partake the Lord's Supper in a UCC church? If we are an inclusive body of Christ, we would have them in our midst, too. Since 1957, when predecessor denominations merged to become the UCC, the UCC proclaims, "There is no barrier for what you understand of the meaning of the Lord's Supper or what your religious experience or faith heritage. You are welcome."

2. If you lived in 1940 Lithuania and had the power to help people in need, what would you have done?

CHILDREN MATTER in the UCC . . . more and more congregations are conscientious about fully including children in worship. Children contribute their skills and personalities throughout the whole worship service. The trend is to reschedule Church school so that it is not at the same hour as worship. In approximately 60–75% UCC congregations, baptized children are welcomed to participate in communion (the earlier tradition was not to allow children to partake of communion until they had completed Confirmation studies).

"Faith supports every breath of life."

4 we are people of covenant

Introduction

"We covenant with the Lord and one another and by ourselves in the presence of God to walk together in all ways." This covenant of the non-separatist congregationally organized Puritan church was adopted in 1629; it is still used by some UCC congregations.

One of the predecessor churches of the present UCC was the first denomination to establish a foreign missionary association in America.

The United Church of Christ has been an active member of the World Council of Churches, the National Council of Churches, and Churches Uniting in Christ.

Covenant today is understood as commitment, agreement or promise. Promises are often made between two or more people who come together and agree upon an issue. Covenants build trust, assurance, and confidence between the parties.

Agreements between people serve to build relationships and understandings among them. Children make promises to friends daily; and amongst family such promises are done automatically without really realizing the implications of those promises. Children take promises seriously and they expect them to come true.

In the UCC, we are a people of covenant. God promises that in Christ we have become his children and we all become one in him. In God's eyes we are all equals, for him there is no color, race or sexual orientation that can separate us from his love. For him, we are a diversity of people just like the rainbow. In other words, we are children of God because we believe in Jesus Christ and in him, God has promised to give us eternal life.

Biblical Foundation

A. *For younger children: Read Genesis 9:12–17 "Noah and the Flood"*

We read in the Bible that God promised to Noah, to all the people, to all the animals, and to the whole creation, a sign. God said that in the clouds God would place a rainbow and that rainbow was going to be the symbol between God and the earth. When the rain comes the rainbow will also appear. It will remind you, the creatures of the earth, and me, of this promise that the earth will never be destroyed by flood again.

Suggestions for wondering about this story with young children:

Oftentimes, children know only half of Noah's story. They know that God told Noah to build an ark and to save a pair of each kind of animals. When all the work had been done and Noah's family, along with the animals, entered the ark, it rained for many days. The waters destroyed the earth! One day the rain stopped and Noah sent out a dove to look for dry land. For several days, the dove returned without bringing a branch from a tree. Noah sent another dove and this time the dove returned with an olive leaf. Noah knew that there was already dry land again.

The second half of the story is often forgotten. It is the part about the covenant between God, the people, and his creation. The rainbow is the symbol that reminds our children and us that the rain will stop and God's promise remains true. The major point of the story is that when promises are made, they are to be kept and not broken — just like God promised to never again completely flood the earth.

- How many times have we promised our child/children something that we can't deliver?

- How many times have our broken promises hurt or disappointed our child/children?

- How can we make promises and keep them?

- Ask your child/children to retell this story to you, their parents, or caregivers.

- What is the important part of the story that you must point out?

- What is a rainbow?

- What is the symbol of the rainbow in our story?

- Who created the rainbow and why?

- How do you know when it is going to rain?

- What do you see in the rainbow? Possible answer: A diversity of colors

- Do you have diversity of colors among your friends?

- Do you have friends of other races/cultures or with different abilities?

- Why do we need promises?

- How can we make promises and keep them?

Suggested activities for families with young children

1. Ask your child/children to draw a rainbow. Help them write these words on their picture, "God's promises are never broken." Keep their rainbow visible in a place that will constantly remind you and them of God's promise.

2. Create a rainbow stick. Gather 24-inch wood sticks. Glue streamers with all the colors of a rainbow to the end of it. Tie it in a bundle and wave your rainbow in the air!

3. Create a rainbow with the sunbeam reflection on glass. Enjoy the prism!

4. Help your child/children to think about promises you can make to each other. Some of them can be penciled in a calendar as a reminder. The promises can be very simple, the simpler, the better. For instance, making one's bed every morning, taking a walk together around the block, helping around the house inside or outside, getting ice cream on a hot summer day.

5. Visit a family member or a friend and together, make something nice happen for yourselves or someone else..

B. For older children: Read Matthew 22:36-39 "The Most Important Commandment"

The people that followed Jesus always had questions for him. This time the question to Jesus was: "Which command (covenant) in the law (Old Testament) is the most important? Jesus answered, "Love God with all your heart, all your spirit and with all your mind." This is the first and the other one is, "Love your neighbor as you love yourself." Jesus said that the most important commandment after loving God is to love others as ourselves. Sounds very simple? Well, if you think about it, it's not as easy as it appears to be.

Suggestions for wondering about this story with older children:

The story for the older group is found in Matthew. Matthew is a disciple of Jesus, in whose Gospel we read the life of Jesus, his sayings, and answers to questions asked of him.

In the New Testament the word "covenant" is a more open-ended word than in the Old Testament. Covenants, in olden times, have to be written, agreements have to be made, conditions have to be established, and obligations have to be expected from both parties.

There is only one commandment in the New Testament that is to love God first with all that we are and then love one another the same way God loves us through Jesus Christ. When we are able to love God, we are able to share that love with family, friends, neighbors, and even strangers. Sometimes we do not know who our neighbor is, but if we want to, we can find out. Our neighbors are our friends and strangers, the familiar and unfamiliar to us, those who are rich and poor. All Jesus wants from us is to share God's love with others by our actions that show caring.

- How have you been a model to your children of this important commandment?

- What did you do?

- How do you show love to others?

- How much do you love God?

- Do you love yourself in the same degree you love others?

- Do you have examples?

- How can you show God's love to other people when they are of different races, cultures, countries, and abilities than you?

- Do you make fun of those different from you?

- Have you thought that the same God, who you love, created them?

- Jesus is saying if we love God with all our being, we are to love those who God created as much as we love and want for ourselves. Can you do this?

Suggested activities for families with older children:

1. As a family, bake homemade cookies and bring them to a family member, a friend, or an old or new neighbor in the neighborhood.

2. Plan to visit the Children's Hospital in your community and take flowers, balloons or sweets to one of the floors.

3. As a family, volunteer to serve food in a local shelter or bring canned goods to a local church, food pantry or shelter.

4. If your child/children have a new classmate from another country, have them go to their local library and reserve books about the country's culture, traditional clothing, and food. Have them share what they learned with their family and classmates.

Family prayer

> Dear God,
>
> May we always stay faithful with our covenant of having a personal relationship with you. Remind us when we go astray. In Jesus name, Amen.

Suggested children's literature to link the theme: "We are a people of covenant"

For young children:

God's Paintbrush by Sandy Eisenberg Sasso, Illustrations by Annette Compton, Woodstock: Jewish Lights Publishing, 2004, ISBN: 1-879045-22-2. To order visit: *www.jewishlights.com.*

Summary

Children speak about God in ways that are different from adults. They ask many questions about God, questions that can be startlingly direct. Oftentimes adults—parents, grandparents and teachers—feel uncomfortable answering them. This book provides a gift of images that nurtures and encourages children in making meaning of their world.

Questions to engage young children about the story:

1. Have you wondered about God? What does God look like?

2. Is God ever sad? Where would you look for God? What does God want you to do?

For older children:

Two Old Women: An Alaska Legend of Betrayal, Courage and Survival by Velma Wallis, Illustrations by Jim Grant, New York: HarperPerenial, 1993, ISBN: 0-06-097584-9. To order visit: *www.HarperCollins.com.*

Summary

Two Old Women, is not a very attractive title for older children. Don't be deceived by it! When we think about loving our families, our neighbors, our friends, and even the stranger as much as we love ourselves, then from that perspective the book becomes an interesting one.

The book is a story of a culture, the Athabascan Indians in the state of Alaska. The tribal legend as stated in the sub-title is about betrayal, courage and survival of two older women. Because winter was coming and the tribe would not have food for everyone, they gave up two of their older women to die in the wilderness. At the end, a lesson is learned by the whole tribe. Read to find out what it is.

Suggestions to engage older children about the story:

1. Read the book only one chapter at a time, then take the time to wonder what is going to happen next.

2. If your child/children likes to journal, have them write their ideas and questions in a journal. Let them share their thoughts with you, their parent/s or caregiver, a sibling or a friend.

3. Go back and read the next chapter. The story will keep you wanting to know more about the discoveries in nature that can be made for survival, hunting wild animals, and building shelter in the snow. Your child/children will learn exciting facts from this tribe.

4. What covenant did the People break with the two old women?

CHILDREN MATTER in the UCC . . . throughout its history as a denomination of four strands of the Christian community, the UCC has placed a strong emphasis on providing programs and resources for the faith formation of children and youth. This includes Church School, youth programs, conference camps and retreats, regional and national events. This has been supported by training and continuing education for church educators.

"Faith supports every breath of life."

5 we thank God by working for a just and loving world

Introduction

From the Lord's Prayer,
"And lead us not into temptation, but deliver us from evil."

The United Church of Christ, in its earliest churches, was the first denomination in America to work for the abolition of slavery.

The Book of Worship says, "Peace with God is inseparable from peace with neighbors."

What Matters is that we thank God by working for a world that is loving and just. How wonderful a thought that God desires a world looking just like God! Imagine a world where all men and women, girls and boys, plants, animals, water and sky are appreciated and protected, and are given space to become everything good that God saw when we were born. Imagine a world where all of creation is cared for, valued, and nurtured.

We all know that our world is not quite the way God really wants it to be. Our waters are polluted. Our air is not always healthy. People seem to be fighting more and more. As people, we are taught to hate, dislike, distrust, tease, or fear those who are different from us. The division is often arbitrary, but for some reason many of us think the division is natural or even the way God wants it. Are there people you have been taught to dislike or be afraid of? When we behave this way, someone always gets hurt. Even in our families, when parents have a favorite child, the other children do not feel loved.

How wonderful to realize that in refusing to hurt each other or the rest of creation, we discover how special we are. How wonderful to think that God has made each of us special, but does not have favorites. God loves every person, every flower, every animal, every planet, and every part of the sky. In fact, God loves when we work to create a world where there is no favoritism, no hurt because of difference, and no walls that keep us from loving each other and treating one another fairly. God loves when we work for a world that is safe and healthy and loves when we see beauty in all of creation and treat it with respect. *What matters is that we thank God by working to create a world that is loving and just.*

Biblical Foundation

A. *For younger children: Read Genesis 1:1–31 "The Creation Story"*

Summary

God created an abundant world for human beings to manage. God saw all creation from plants, animals, and humans were good. God said, "See, I have given you every plant yielding seed that is upon the face of all the earth, and every tree with seed in its fruit; you shall have them for food. And to every beast of the earth, and to every bird of the air, and to everything that creeps on the earth, everything that has the breath of life, I have given every green plant for food." God wanted us to take care of our world.

Suggestions for wondering about this story with young children:

From our Bible reading, God has given us a wonderful world. We have been entrusted to take care of this world.

- Have we followed God's instruction faithfully, to be kind and gentle to our world?

- How have we been poor caretakers of our surroundings?

- What about our relationship with one another and with the animals?

Suggested activities for families with young children

1. Take the time to go to your local zoo.

2. Think about these animals as one of God's creation in the book of Genesis.

3. Play a game of who can name the most animals.

B. *For older children: Read Genesis 25: 24–28; Genesis 27:1–41 "Esau and Jacob"*

Summary

The story of twin brothers Jacob and Esau is a story of favoritism. The father, Isaac, loved Esau more than Jacob because Esau was born first. Esau loved his father's cooking. Their mother, Rebekah, loved Jacob more than Esau, perhaps because he was younger or because of his disposition to spend more time with her. Because of favoritism, it caused a lot of deceit, anger, sadness, hurt and fighting between the brothers. Even though it hurt, later in life Jacob did the same thing in his own family, causing more hurt almost to the point of death.

Suggestions for wondering about this story for children:

- Do you feel that there is favoritism in your family? If so, talk about how it feels and name ways to stop it.

- Starting with your family and community, can you think of ways to help make our world more loving and just?

- Are there people who are different from you who you dislike or fear? Why?

- Who or what do you fear? Why?

Suggested activities for families with both younger and older children:

1. Take a walk outside. Find six different things that God created. How do these things depend on one another for life? Do you think that God loves and appreciates any of them more than the others?

2. Is there an organization in your community or school that is helping to create a just and loving world?

3. Look around your school or neighborhood. Take notice of the

people that are bullied, mistreated or left to be by themselves. Why do you think people treat them differently? Is it because they look different, have a different way of speaking or have they chose to behave in ways that others find uncomfortable?

Do not try to help them, instead, get to know them. Appreciate that which is special about them. Be conscious of the struggles that you have in common. An aboriginal woman once said, "If you have come to help me, then, you may turn and go home. But if your struggle is connected to my struggle, then come and let us work together."

Family Prayer

Dear God,

Please forgive us for allowing differences to cause hurtful division. Help us to know that different does not mean deficient. Please help us to see each other and all of creation through your eyes and heart. Thank you for making us special so that we are able to help make our families, communities, and this world loving and just. In Jesus' name we pray. Amen.

Help us God to see our world as your love would make it:

- a place where the weak are protected and none go hungry or poor

- a place where the good things in life are shared and everyone can enjoy them

- a place where different skin colors and languages help each other and give us the right words and actions to build it.

Suggested children's literature to link the theme: "We thank God by working for a just and loving world"

For young children:

What If the Zebras Lost their Stripes? by John Reitano, Illustrations by William Haines, New York/Mahwah: Paulist Press, 1998, ISBN: 0-8091-6649-6. To order visit: *www.paulistpress.com.*

Summary

This is a story that helps us to understand that we are all brothers and sisters in God's eyes. We might be different colors, different sizes, different religions, but we are all important to God. Some zebras lost black stripes and other lost white stripes. What is left are Zebras separated by color—either all white or all black. All the black zebras were on one side and all the white zebras were together. Their separation began to cause problems that never existed before. So you see God never meant for the zebras to be separated, so, God created zebras to have black and white stripes on their bodies!

Questions to engage young children about the story:

1. Do you wonder how the Zebras treated each other when they had their stripes?

2. Do you wonder how the Zebras treated each other when they lost their stripes?

For young and older children:

The Great Kapok Tree: A Tale of the Amazon Rainforest by Lynne Cherry, San Diego: Voyager Books Harcourt Inc., 1990, ISBN: 0-15-202614-2. To order visit: *www.Amazon.com.*

Summary

In the Amazon rainforest, it is always hot. And in that heat everything grows, and grows, and grows. The top of the trees in the rainforest are called the canopy. The canopy is a sunny place that touches the sky. The animals that live there like lots of light. Colorful parrots fly from tree to tree. Monkeys leap from branch to branch. The bottom of the rainforest is called the understory. The animals living in the understory like darkness. There, silent snakes curl around hanging vines. Graceful jaguars watch and wait.

And in this steamy environment, the great Kapok tree shoots up through the forest and emerges above the canopy.

This is a story of a community of animals that live in one such tree in the rainforest. One day, the animals see a man chopping down a great Kapok tree. Exhausted from his labors, he puts down his ax and rests. As he sleeps, the animals that live in the tree plead with him not to destroy their world.

Questions to engage children about the story:

1. Think about the beautiful living and non-living things that exist in our world. Why do we hear news about how the earth has become polluted? What does that mean?

2. What do you think the man was planning to do with the Kapok tree?

3. In what ways have we contributed to the destruction of the rainforest?

4. How can we keep our promise to live in a loving and just world? God entrusted us to care for the world. God created a beautiful world.

The Skin I'm In by Pat Thomas, Illustrations by Lesley Harker, Hauppauge: Barron's Educational Series, Inc., 2003, ISBN: 13: 987-0-7641-2459-4; 10: 0-7641-2459-5. To order visit: *www.barronseduc.com.*

Summary

Racial discrimination is cruel—and especially to children. This story encourages kids to accept and be comfortable with differences of skin color and other racial characteristics among their friends and in themselves.

Questions and suggestions to engage children about the story:

1. What do you know about your family's history?

2. What is the variety of skin colors that people come in?

3. Have you ever been bullied because of your skin color?

4. Have you ever seen anyone bullied because of this?

5. How did it make you feel?

6. Where do we start to make this world just and loving?

Note to Parents: "Racism is a complex issue that brings up a wide range of emotions in all of us."[9] According to the definition used in the UCC, "*Racism* is racial prejudice plus power. Racism is the intentional or unintentional use of power to isolate, separate and exploit others. This use of power is based on a belief in superior origin, identity of supposed racial characteristics. Racism confers certain privileges on and defends the dominant group, which in turn sustains and perpetuates racism. Both consciously and unconsciously, racism is enforced and maintained by the legal, cultural, religious, educational, economical, political and military institutions of societies. Racism is more than just a personal attitude. It is the institutionalized form of that attitude. It is both overt and covert."

There, however, must be some word of caution in labeling a selected group of people as racist. From the standpoint of people with class, power, and privilege, there is the assumption that everyone in the world can be racist to one another. But from the standpoint of people who have no class, power or privilege, they can only express prejudice because it is not accompanied with class, power or privilege status whether it is targeted to those with power or without power. They have prejudicial attitudes, but they can't be called racists. In other countries, people with class, power, and privilege can oppress their own same skin color, they are "classist/elitist" not racist. But the ones whose expression of prejudices to all nonwhite people accompanied with class, power, and privilege, can be racist. The shortest way to describe racism/classism is having prejudice plus power!

For older children:

Friends from the Other Side, Amigos Del Otro Lado by Gloria Anzaldua, Illustrations by Consuelo Mendez, San Francisco: Children's Book Press, 1993, ISBN–13: 978-0-89239-130-1. To order visit: *www. childrensbookpress.com* or call: 1-800-788-3123.

Summary

This is a story of a young boy and his mother who cross the border from Mexico to Rio Grande to Texas in search of a new life. "Prietita," a brave young Mexican American girl, defends Joaquin from neighborhood kids that taunt him with shouts of "Mojado" or "Wetback". The girl provides a hiding place to protect Joaquin and his mother.

Questions/suggestion to engage children about the story:

1. Many come to America to seek a better life for their family. Do you think that it is good to help the mother and son hide from the border patrol? Are we to help them even if they did not come to the U.S. legally? Is it a good thing to do? Or should we deliver them to the police?

2. What is the just thing to do in this story?

3. What can you say about Prietita?

4. Would you be as courageous as her when she protected Joaquin from the bullies?

5. Is the behavior of the American boys towards Joaquin an example of racist behavior? Discuss it with your family.

Since many cross the US border from Mexico to find work, while crossing the river, they get wet, so they get the name *"mojado"* or wetback.

Note to parents: This is a sensitive issue that is going on in our country, that is, the topic of immigration and illegal immigrants. Keep your discussion as simple as possible. Focus on the human situation of youngsters caught by the decisions of their parents. This may also spark an interesting conversation why people want to come to the USA even by illegal means.

CHILDREN MATTER in the UCC... in front of our children we talk a lot and do a lot that addresses the injustices in our community. As we teach our children, we raise issues of fairness and responsibility of the citizens in our nation. We create activities and projects to help children learn ways to be proactive in working for equal opportunity and inclusion of all people.

"Faith supports every breath of life."

6 we listen for a still-speaking God

Introduction

Reinhold Neibuhr, a UCC theologian, composed the Serenity Prayer, "God give us grace to accept with serenity the things that cannot be changed, the courage to change the things that should be changed and the wisdom to distinguish the one from the other." 1943

The Kansas City statement of faith of the Congregational Churches in 1913, affirmed, We are united in striving to know the will of God, . . . and to walk in the ways of the Lord made known or to be made known to us."

We expect that when we listen, God continues to speak to us, knowing that God cares for us even now, as from the beginning of all time. God didn't just sit back after the creation event and forget about our world and the people in it. Rather, God has a vested interest in what we are doing about caring for the earth and its people. Our God is a "hands on God", continually creating and re-creating and expecting and enlisting our participation in it. In this same way, we expect new understandings and meanings to come to us by God's intentional communication with humanity.

God speaks to us in a myriad of ways. We must always be attuned to the possibility that, at any moment, God has more to say to us. There is an historical quote that we cherish from the pastor of the earliest Pilgrim ancestors when he gave this advice before their venture to this continent. Pilgrim pastor, John Robinson, stated:

> *"I charge you before God and His blessed angels that you follow me no further than you have seen me follow the Lord Jesus Christ. If God revealed anything to you by any other instrument of His, be as ready to receive it as you were to receive any truth from my ministry, for I am very persuaded the Lord hath more truth and light to break forth from His holy word."*
>
> —John Robinson in his farewell address in Delfshaven,
> The Netherlands, to the first Pilgrim setting sail in 1620

It has been observed that history has been recorded by the victors in our society, carefully described by those who came out on top of whatever conflict—however major or subtle. So it can be said that little has been written about the experience of those "who lost the war", or those who were bussed out of their neighborhoods, etc., or those whose lives were broken, property and possessions plundered, spirits dashed, hope crushed—while the opponents take their laps around the field. Only on rare occasions have the writings of the oppressed survived so we might read them today.

It has been noted by contemporary historians that the immigration of European Pilgrims and Puritans has not always been accurate. So, it becomes necessary for historians and authors who are committed to justice and fairness in this world, to research, and then to pause and reflect on the past. It is important that they do a corrective on the hurtful words misspoken. New descriptions may need to be written that tell the stories from other perspectives. So that it can be through the talents of people of integrity who seek truth, God can speak to us today by the presentation of the other side(s) of stories that have heretofore been told unjustly.

Biblical Foundation

For both younger and older children: Read 1 Samuel 3:1–24 "God Calling Samuel"

Summary

The Scripture reference is the familiar story of the boy Samuel. In gratitude to God for giving her a son, the child's mother, Hannah, presents him back at the Temple. Samuel lives in the Temple and serves Eli, the Priest. These verses reveal God's persistence when trying to get through to Samuel.

In a sometimes humorous and at the same time, serious exchange with the boy Samuel, God can be heard repeating the call to Samuel, and Samuel repeatedly is confused. God calls again and again, but Samuel cannot figure out the source of the voice. Finally, after several tries and some instruction from Eli, the Priest, God gets through to Samuel who figures out that God is trying to tell him something. Samuel understood and he told God that he was ready to listen.

You might tell the story in your own words this way.

One night when Samuel was still a small child, he was lying on his bed in the Temple, trying to get to sleep. He heard a voice calling, "Samuel, Samuel". Samuel thought it was the old priest, Eli. Samuel answered back and said, "Here I am".

Eli woke from a sound sleep and told Samuel to go back to bed as it wasn't he who was calling to him.

This happened a second time, and again Eli told Samuel to go to back to bed.

Finally, Eli, the Priest, figured out that it was God calling to Samuel. He told Samuel what to say if it should happen again.

The third time that God called, Samuel understood what was happening and he replied to God by saying, "Speak God, for your servant is listening."

Suggestions for wondering about this story for parents and caregivers:

Eager that truth is told and that justice prevail; through the ages, God delegates to faithful people the task of communicating truths, visions, etc. in simple honest, straightforward ways. God's people can now comprehend them. Sometimes, as in the case of young Samuel, God even chooses a child to tell the news that needs to be told. We all know times when we learn more from our children than from all of our study—reading of experts and personal observation.

This text reminds us of God's persistence with us as well. Sometimes we think that God will not have anything particular to say to us. Sometimes we think and feel that we are not important enough for God to need our help. Sometimes we don't know how to listen and to watch for God's presence in our lives. Because we feel badly about past mistakes, we assume God will have no reason to call to us, the way God called to Samuel.

A great spiritual leader and Christian from the fourteenth century, St. Teresa of Avila, reminds us that God needs us, and that WE are God's hands.

"God has no body on earth but yours,
no hands but yours,
no feet but yours.
Your are the eyes through which the opportunity and the need
For God's compassion will first be seen;
yours are the feet with which God is to go about doing good;
and yours are the hands with which God is to bless us now."

Once we hear God's call to us, we can be busy doing God's work, helping God to care for and love the people on the earth, to work for justice where injustice remains unchallenged and to care for the earth itself.

Suggestions for wondering about this story with children

Parents and caregivers often may need to repeat their words several times to children before they are really heard or understood. Sometimes friends have to find alternative ways to say something important to another person in order that the person will pay attention. On other occasions, people may have to see a picture, read a map, read words, dance, run, jump or engage in a physical activity in order to learn and understand something new.

Eager to get the attention of humankind, God sometimes has to continue repeating God's call until it is heard in a myriad of different ways.

- If God called in the night, imagine with your child what God's voice might sound like.

- Why do you think Samuel thought it was Eli calling him?

- How do you think that Eli knew it was God's voice?

- How might we listen for God to speak to us?

- Epictetus, the ancient philosopher said: "Nature has given us two ears and one mouth so that we can listen twice as much as we speak." What might that mean?

Suggested activities for families with children:

1. *Make listening shakers:* Use 10 plastic film canisters to make five pairs of Listening Shakers. Place materials that make a different sound in each pair. You might use such things as rocks, pennies, sand, and paper clips. If you want to make them self-correcting, place an identifying symbol on the bottom of each pair—yellow dots on the penny shakers and green dots on the sand, for example. After shaking each container and matching them, the child can turn them over to see if they are correctly matched.

2. *Listening for God:* Ask your child how s/he thinks we should try to listen for God. Do we need to be still to hear God? Can we hear God in a noisy city or when the band plays a loud song? Do we need to close our eyes to hear God? (Parents should be careful not to reject the ideas that children have about listening for God. God still speaks in many ways to God's people. Who are we to discount any variations a child might suggest?

Family Prayer

Dear God,

Be with us in our talking and in our listening as we listen for your call. We thank you for creating us and loving us. We are grateful that your presence is always with us. Help us to listen with our ears, and our hearts, and our minds for the message you might have for us. Help us to learn how to be your faithful people. Empower us, O God, to spread your love in the world. In Jesus name we pray. Amen

Suggested children's literature that links the theme: "We listen for a still-speaking God"

For younger children:

Nickommoh! A Thanksgiving Celebration by Jackie French Koller, Illustrations by Marcia Sewall, New York: Atheneum Books for Young Readers, 1999. ISBN-10: 0689810946, ISBN-13: 978-0689810947. To order visit: *www.SimonSaysKids.com.*

Summary

The storybook describes *Nickommoh,* the annual thanksgiving celebration typical of those celebrated by Native American Indians in the New England area for hundreds of years before the arrival of the Mayflower Pilgrims.

Questions to engage parents and caregivers:

Consider how this story differs from other accounts written for children about the first arrival of the Mayflower Pilgrims. Why do you think it is included here?

For younger children:

1. How many native people do you think came to the feast?

2. What would we have to do to build a shelter like theirs?

3. Do you think that Pilgrims came to the feast?

4. Do you think that the native children and the pilgrim children had a good time playing together that day?

5. What other things do you wonder about this story?

For older children:

Mayflower 1620—A New Look at a Pilgrim Voyage by Peter Arenstam, John Kemp, and Catherine O'Neill Grace. Photography by Sissse Brimberg and Cotton Coulson. Washington: National Geographic Society, 2003, ISBN 10: 0792261399, ISBN 13: 978-0792261391. To order visit: *www.nationalgeographic.com.*

Summary

This is a text for older children that also serve to do some correctives on the past accounts of Pilgrim life before and after their arrival at Plymouth. Published by National Geographic, the book is illustrated with photographs taken during a special voyage of the Mayflower II taken for this sole purpose. The book takes a fresh look on the voyage of the Mayflower and points out earlier distortions and omissions of the story.

Question to engage parents and caregivers

1. What unfamiliar information did you find that might add to your child's understanding of the Pilgrim story?

For older children:

1. Do you think the ship really looked like this reproduction?

2. Why do you think that some books don't tell that the people didn't always get along with each other?

3. What would it be like to leave your family and never be sure when you'd see them again?

4. What other things do you wonder about this story?

Suggested activities for families with children:

1. If possible, plan a trip to Plimoth Plantation in Plymouth, Massachusetts. It is a great place to go in the summer. It is fun for children as well as instructional. The Mayflower is available

at the coast for tours as well. Or visit the Plimoth Plantation website, to see photographs of the reproduction houses and the Indian village. Resources are available online: *www.plimoth.org*

2. Consider visiting other living history museums in your geographic area, particularly those which feature Native American ruins, artifacts or re-creation of native villages, anywhere in the country. Help children to learn about the wide variety of Native American cultures in our country. Help them listen for all sides of the stories told.

3. Buy some books that give good lessons about understanding people of a different cultural heritage than your own. You might even buy extra copies to give your local library or your children's school.

4. Find out more, by Internet search about the event of the "Amistad" journey. Or borrow the movie at your local library.

5. For one week, encourage and help your children to keep a journal or record of all the images that you observe on television that have some message that makes you think about God speaking to you.

CHILDREN MATTER in the UCC… the style of teaching our children is usually designed to help them learn the joy of inquiry, the freedom of personal opinion and the responsibility of being informed about the issues of faith. This contrasts to an earlier style, and those used by other denominations where memorizations of Scripture and adherence to dogma is the predominant style. Throughout its history in the USA, the United Church of Christ has been involved in the creation of many schools and colleges, including those serving marginalized people within our society.

"Faith supports every breath of life."

notes

1. Catherine Stonehouse, *Joining Children on the Spiritual Journey*. (Grand Rapids: Baker Books, 1998)p. 188

2. Ibid., 188

3. Ibid.,188

4. Virgilio Elizondo, *The Future Is Mestizo*. (Boulder: University Press of Colorado, 2000) p. 81

5. Ibid., 83

6. Ibid., 83

7. New knowledge has come to light about our DNA. According to research, if we are to investigate our DNA identity, we will find out that we have originated from Africa. For more information, visit the *www.PBS.org/Race*. Read about the exhibition, "Race: Are We So Different?" developed by the American Anthropological Association in collaboration with the Science Museum of Minnesota. Visit their website for schedules of exhibition in your State. View: *http://www.cmnh.org/siteRACE.aspx*

8. Virgilio Elizondo, *The Future Is Mestizo*. (Boulder: University Press of Colorado, 2000) p.83

9. Pat Thomas, *The Skin I'm In*. (Hauppauge: Barron's, 2003) p. 28

recommended reading

Bisson, Julie, *Celebrate! An Anti-Bias Guide to Enjoying Holidays in Early Childhood Programs.* (St. Paul: Red Leaf Press, 1997)

Granahan, Louise Margaret, *Children's Books that Nurture the Spirit.* (British Columbia: Northstone, 2003)